September/Septiembre

By/Por Robyn Brode

Reading Consultant/Consultora de lectura: Linda Cornwell, Literacy Connections Consulting/consultora de lectoescritura

WEEKLY READER® PUBLISHING

Please visit our web site at **www.garethstevens.com**.
For a free catalog describing our list of high-quality books, call 1-800-542-2595 (USA)
or 1-800-387-3178 (Canada). Our fax: 1-877-542-2596

Library of Congress Cataloging-in-Publication Data

[September. Spanish & English]
September / by Robyn Brode ; reading consultant, Linda Cornwell — Septiembre / por
Robyn Brode ; consultora de lectura, Linda Cornwell
p. cm. — (Months of the year — Meses del año)
English and Spanish in parallel text.
Includes bibliographical references and index.
ISBN-10: 1-4339-1937-0   ISBN-13: 978-1-4339-1937-4 (lib. bdg.)
ISBN-10: 1-4339-2114-6   ISBN-13: 978-1-4339-2114-8 (softcover)
1. September—Juvenile literature. 2. Holidays—United States—Juvenile literature.
3. Autumn—United States—Juvenile literature. I. Cornwell, Linda. II. Title. III. Title: Septiembre.
GT4803.B67318   2010
394.264—dc22   2009013988

This edition first published in 2010 by
Weekly Reader® Books
An Imprint of Gareth Stevens Publishing
1 Reader's Digest Road
Pleasantville, NY 10570-7000 USA

Copyright © 2010 by Gareth Stevens, Inc.

Executive Managing Editor: Lisa M. Herrington
Senior Editors: Barbara Bakowski, Jennifer Magid-Schiller
Designer: Jennifer Ryder-Talbot
Translators: Tatiana Acosta and Guillermo Gutiérrez

Photo Credits: Cover, back cover, title © Fancy Photography/Veer; p. 7 © Andrejs Pidjass/
Shutterstock; pp. 9, 21 © Ariel Skelley/Weekly Reader; p. 11 © Lori Sparkia/Shutterstock;
p. 13 © Monkey Business Images/Shutterstock; p. 15 © Evok20/Shutterstock; p. 17 © Masterfile/
Radius Images; p. 19 © Sonya Etchison/Shutterstock

Printed in the United States of America

1 2 3 4 5 6 7 8 9 10 11 10 09

Table of Contents/Contenido

Boldface words appear in the glossary.

Las palabras en **negrita** aparecen en el glosario.

Welcome to September!

September is the ninth month of the year.

September has 30 days.

– – – – – – – – – –

¡Bienvenidos a septiembre!

Septiembre es el noveno mes del año.

Septiembre tiene 30 días.

Months of the Year/Meses del año

Month/Mes	Number of Days/ Días en el mes
1 January/Enero	31
2 February/Febrero	28 or 29*/28 ó 29*
3 March/Marzo	31
4 April/Abril	30
5 May/Mayo	31
6 June/Junio	30
7 July/Julio	31
8 August/Agosto	31
9 **September/Septiembre**	**30**
10 October/Octubre	31
11 November/Noviembre	30
12 December/Diciembre	31

*February has an extra day every fourth year./Febrero tiene un día extra cada cuatro años.

In September, summer ends and **fall** begins. Fall usually begins on September 22. Fall is also called autumn.

– – – – – – – – – –

En septiembre, se acaba el verano y empieza el **otoño**. Normalmente, el otoño empieza el 22 de septiembre.

In some places, school begins in September.

– – – – – – – – –

En algunos lugares, la escuela empieza en septiembre.

 When do you go back to school?
– – – – – – –
¿En qué mes vuelves a la escuela?

Special Celebrations

The first Monday in September is **Labor Day**. This holiday honors people who work.

— — — — — — — — —

Celebraciones especiales

El primer lunes de septiembre es *Labor Day* (Día del Trabajo). Es una fiesta en honor a los trabajadores.

Hispanic Heritage Month begins on September 15. It lasts until October 15. It is a time to celebrate Hispanic **traditions**.

— — — — — — — — — —

El **Mes de la Herencia Hispana** empieza el 15 de septiembre y dura hasta el 15 de octubre. En él se festejan las **tradiciones** de la cultura hispana.

Fall Fun

Many people play football in September. Some people like to watch football games.

- - - - - - - - - -

Diversión de otoño

En septiembre, muchas personas juegan al fútbol americano. A algunas personas les gusta mirar los partidos.

 What is your favorite sport to play or to watch?

¿Qué deporte te gusta más practicar? ¿Qué deporte te gusta ver?

In many places, apple season begins in September. People pick apples from trees.

— — — — — — — — — —

En muchos lugares, la temporada de las manzanas comienza en septiembre. Mucha gente va a recoger manzanas de los árboles.

apples/
manzanas

When September ends, it is time for October to begin.

- - - - - - - - - -

Cuando septiembre termina, empieza octubre.

Glossary/Glosario

fall: the season between summer and winter, when the days get shorter and the weather gets cooler. It is also called autumn.

Hispanic Heritage Month: a special time from September 15 to October 15 that celebrates Hispanic traditions

Labor Day: a holiday that honors workers. It is celebrated on the first Monday in September.

traditions: customs or practices handed down by people

— — — — — — — —

Labor Day **(Día del Trabajo):** fiesta en honor a los trabajadores. Se celebra el primer lunes de septiembre.

Mes de la Herencia Hispana: periodo que dura del 15 de septiembre al 15 de octubre, en el que se celebran las tradiciones hispanas

otoño: la estación del año entre el verano y el invierno, en la que los días se acortan y el tiempo se vuelve más fresco

tradiciones: costumbres o maneras de hacer las cosas que se transmiten de generación en generación

For More Information/Más información

Books/Libros

Going to School/De camino a la escuela. My Day at School/Mi día en la escuela (series). Joanne Mattern (Gareth Stevens Publishing, 2007)

How Apple Trees Grow/Cómo crecen los manzanos. How Plants Grow/Cómo crecen las plantas (series). Joanne Mattern (Gareth Stevens Publishing, 2006)

Web Sites/Páginas web

Hispanic Heritage Month/Mes de la Herencia Hispana
www.factmonster.com/spot/hhm1.html
Learn all about Hispanic Heritage Month, including famous firsts by Hispanic Americans./Conozcan todos los detalles sobre el Mes de la Herencia Hispana, incluyendo información sobre famosos estadounidenses de origen hispano.

Labor Day Activities/Actividades de *Labor Day*
www.apples4theteacher.com/holidays/labor-day
Find coloring pages, crafts, and Labor Day history./Encuentren hojas para colorear y manualidades, y conozcan la historia de *Labor Day*.

Index/Índice

About the Author

Robyn Brode has been a teacher, a writer, and an editor in the book publishing field for many years. She earned a bachelor's degree in English literature from the University of California, Berkeley.

- - - - - - - - -

Información sobre la autora

Robyn Brode ha sido maestra, escritora y editora de libros durante muchos años. Obtuvo su licenciatura en literatura inglesa en la Universidad de California, Berkeley.